HOW MACHINES CHANGED CULTURES

INDUSTRIAL REVOLUTION FOR KIDS

HISTORY FOR KIDS

TIMELINES OF HISTORY FOR KIDS

6TH GRADE SOCIAL STUDIES

BABY PROFESSOR
EDUCATION KIDS

Speedy Publishing LLC

40 E. Main St. #1156

Newark, DE 19711

www.speedypublishing.com

Copyright 2018

In this book, we're going to talk about the history of the Industrial Revolution. So, let's get right to it!

The Industrial Revolution is the name that represents an era in history. It began in Great Britain and spread throughout Europe and then the United States. The word "revolution" here doesn't mean a war. Instead, it means a huge shift in culture. Prior to this time, textiles and fabrics were made at home.

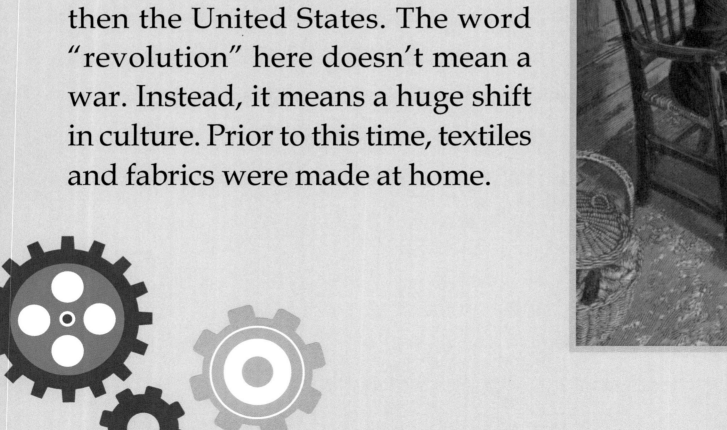

HOME TEXTILE WORKSHOP IN PROVINCIAL GREAT BRITAIN

The advent of new machinery made it possible for people to mass-produce textiles and other products. Machines also revolutionized the way that farming was done. Instead of cutting down harvests with a sickle, farmers began to use machinery like mechanical reapers.

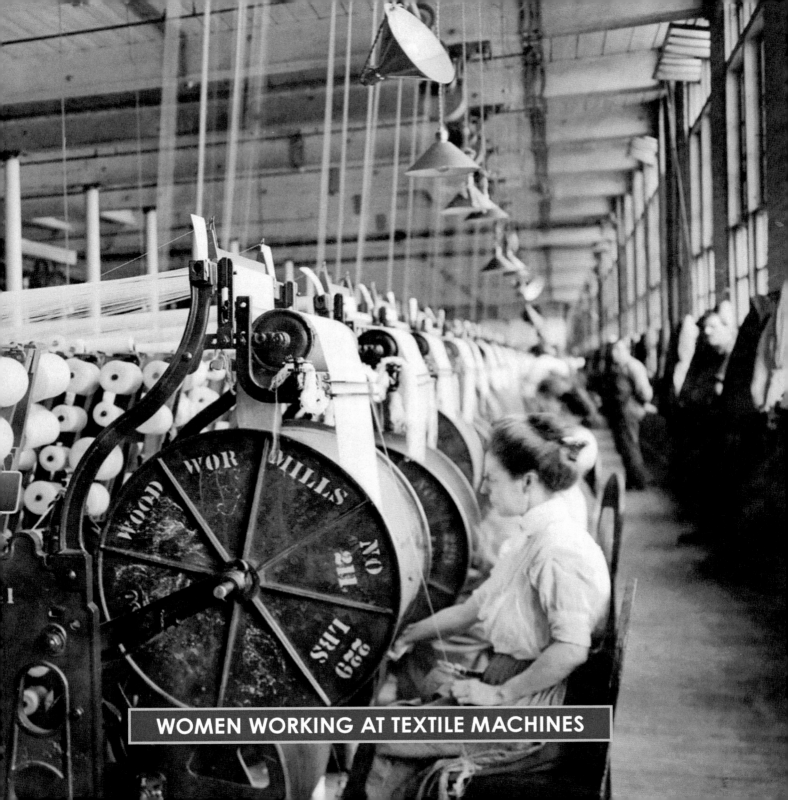

WOMEN WORKING AT TEXTILE MACHINES

WHERE DID THIS ERA BEGIN?

Great Britain was the first place where this shift in culture happened. This took place in the late 1700s and was spurred on by new inventions in the making of textiles. Women were making thread, fabric, and garments at home, which was a time-consuming and arduous process. With the new machinery, it was possible to mass-produce all the steps needed to make garments.

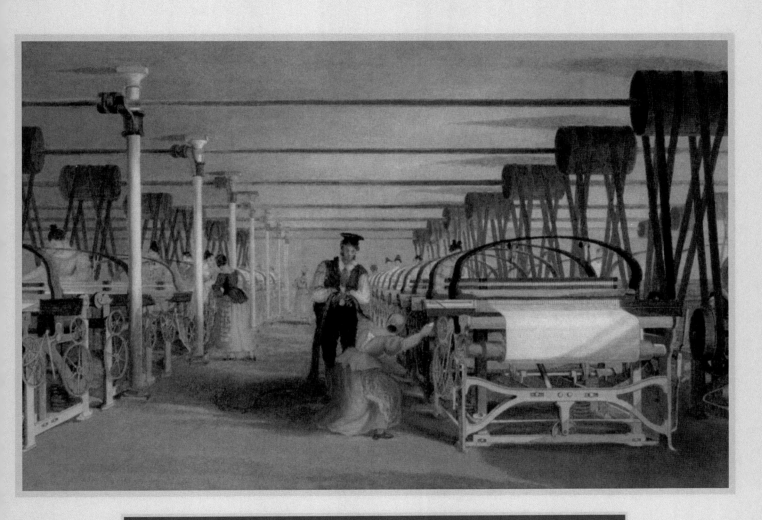

POWER LOOM WEAVING IN A COTTON MILL

TEXTILE MACHINE

At the beginning, water power provided the necessary energy, but soon there was electricity. Great Britain was rich in the resources of both coal as well as iron, which made it possible to power and build these new machines.

HOW LONG DID IT LAST?

The Industrial Revolution lasted for about two centuries. Historians generally study it in two separate phases: the first and the second.

INDUSTRIAL REVOLUTION

SPINNING JENNY

The First Industrial Revolution

The first phase began in the late 1700s and continued to the middle of the 1800s. During this time, the textile industry transformed from spinning and sewing in rural homes to mass production in urban factories. The invention of steam energy made this possible. Also, the inventions of the spinning jenny, the spinning mule, and the cotton gin all made it possible to mass-produce textiles.

The Second Industrial Revolution

The next portion of the era lasted from the middle of the 1800s to the beginning of the 1900s. This was the era when new technologies came into play. The inexpensive production of quality steel made possible by Henry Bessemer, the advent of electrical power stations, and the invention of the assembly line all increased the industrial power of Europe, Great Britain, and the United States.

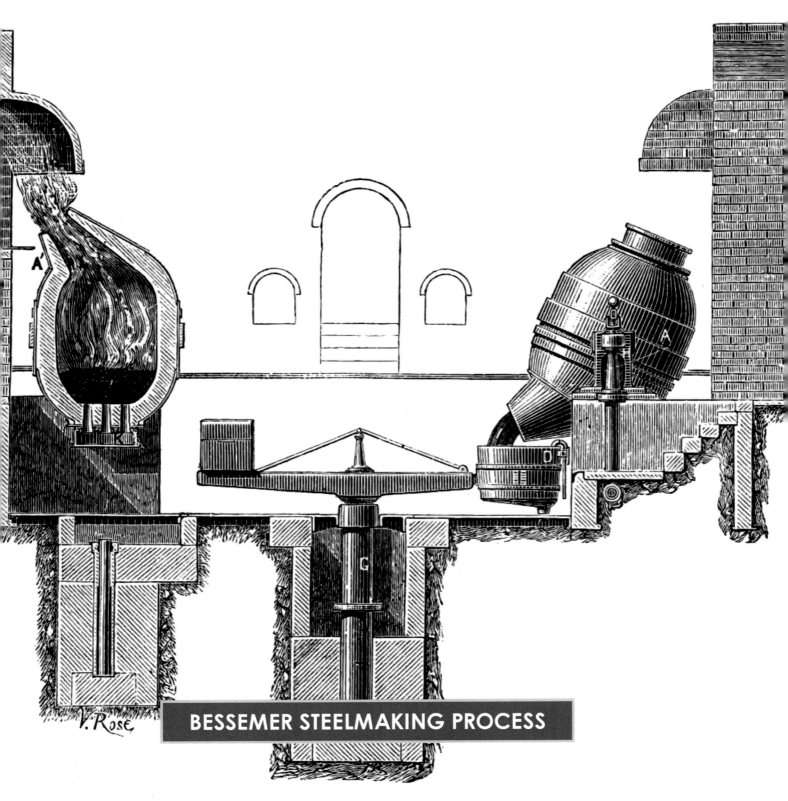

BESSEMER STEELMAKING PROCESS

WHEN DID THIS CHANGE HAPPEN IN THE UNITED STATES?

Many historians believe that the start of the Industrial Revolution in the United States can be traced to the establishment of Slater's Mill in Rhode Island, which took place in the year 1793. Slater had learned the new textile techniques in

England and then brought his knowledge to the United States, which was a relatively new country. A century later, the United States was the most industrialized country worldwide.

WHAT TYPES OF CULTURAL CHANGES WERE THERE?

Prior to this era, most people lived on farms. However, with new jobs being created in the cities, people moved there to get work. Unfortunately, the cities were not equipped to deal with the influx of population. The working conditions were very poor. Workers often lived in tight quarters that were unclean and overcrowded.

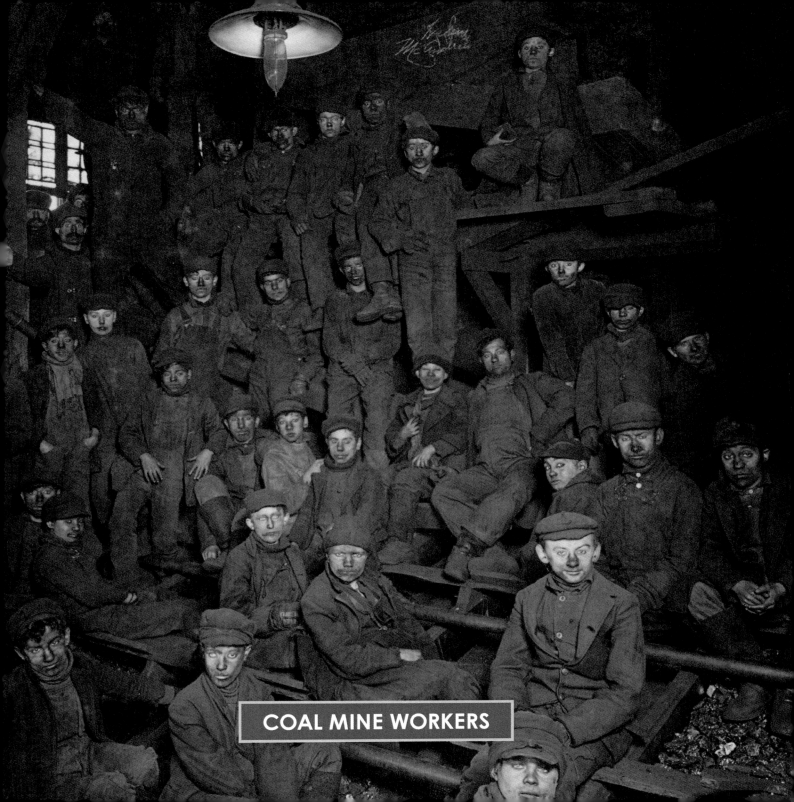

COAL MINE WORKERS

YOUNG BOYS AND GIRLS WORKING IN THE SPINNING ROOM

It took a long time for conditions to improve for workers. Working conditions in the factories were often very hazardous. People, even children, worked very long hours. Eventually, by the end of the 1900s, laws were put into place to protect workers.

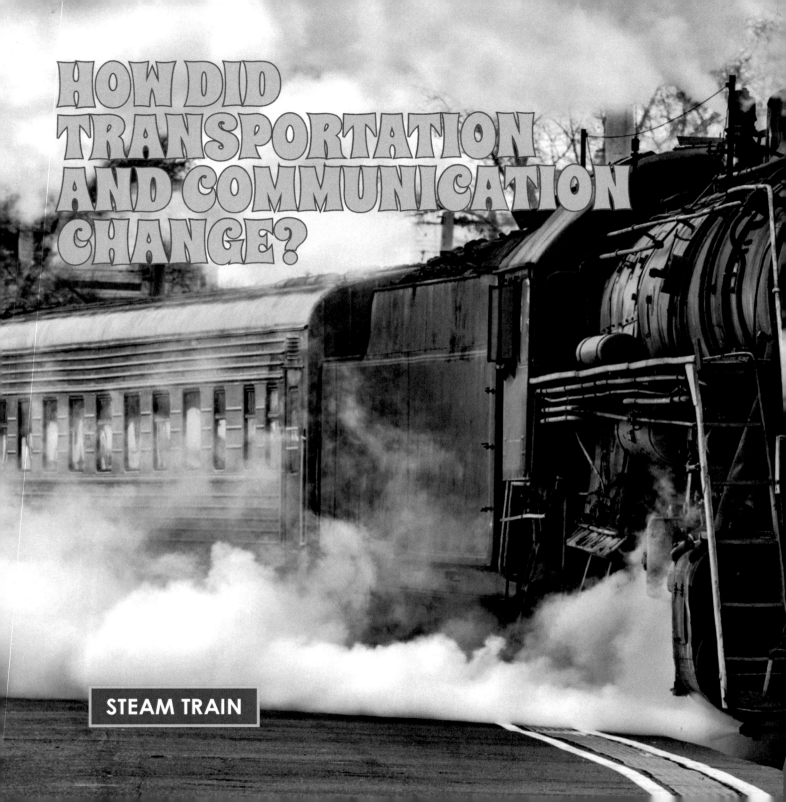

HOW DID TRANSPORTATION AND COMMUNICATION CHANGE?

STEAM TRAIN

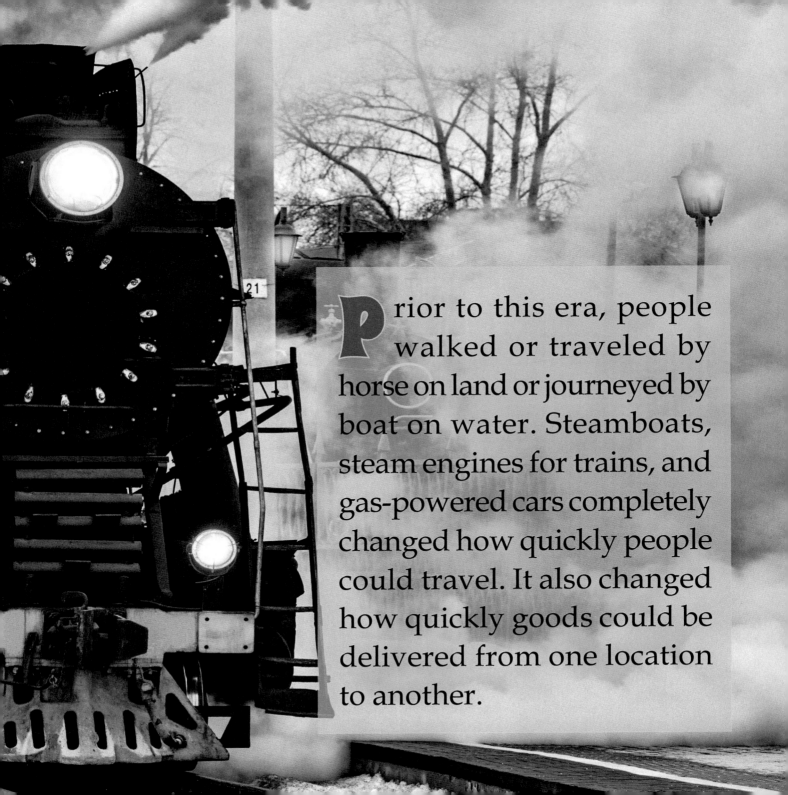

Prior to this era, people walked or traveled by horse on land or journeyed by boat on water. Steamboats, steam engines for trains, and gas-powered cars completely changed how quickly people could travel. It also changed how quickly goods could be delivered from one location to another.

TIMELINE OF MAJOR EVENTS DURING THE INDUSTRIAL REVOLUTION

Here are some of the major events during the first and second Industrial Revolutions.

1712

Thomas Newcomen creates the first steam engine that has practical applications. Steam power is an important source of energy for machine power during the Industrial Revolution.

1760

The age described as the First Industrial Revolution starts in 1760. The production of textile in the country of Great Britain moves from manual work in rural homes to factory production in the city.

1764

The spinning jenny, invented by James Hargreaves, changes the way textiles are made. Workers can create threads by using numerous spools simultaneously.

TEXTILE WEAVING FACTORY

SPINNING MULE

1779

The spinning mule, devised by Samuel Crompton, was a combination of the spinning jenny and the water frame. That was why it was called a "mule" because it was a hybrid of two different machines. It sped up the time required to spin cotton and other fabrics.

1781

James Watt takes out patents for a steam engine with improved features. This new steam engine is ideal for factories as well as for powering trains and steamboats.

STEAM BOAT

COTTON GIN

1793

The first mill, established by Samuel Slater, is opened in the state of Rhode Island, marking the official beginning of the Industrial Revolution in the United States.

1793

The cotton gin, invented by Eli Whitney, makes cotton processing much more efficient by separating the fibers of cotton from the cottonseeds.

1807

Robert Fulton begins the first steamboat business with his flagship boat called the *Clermont*.

1811

A group of citizens called the Luddites cause uprisings in Great Britain. They protest the changes of the Industrial Revolution by breaking machinery in factories.

ROBERT FULTON'S FIRST STEAMSHIP

ERIE CANAL

1824

In Great Britain, workers gather together in legalized trade unions.

1825

The construction of the Erie Canal is finished. It provides a route from the Great Lakes to the city of New York and out to the Atlantic Ocean.

MODERN MECHANICAL REAPER

1831

Cyrus McCormick creates the first mechanical reaper. It made it possible for farmers to harvest crops by machine instead of using hand tools such as the sickle.

STEEL PLOW

1837

The steel plow, invented by blacksmith John Deere, made it possible for farmers to work more efficiently. It was difficult to scrape the sticky soil off of previous plows, which were made of iron.

WOMAN SENDING MORSE CODE USING TELEGRAPH

1844

Samuel Morse creates the telegraph. The new invention allows people to send coded messages over long distances.

1844

Vulcanized rubber, invented by Charles Goodyear in 1844, is a hardened rubber that doesn't melt. Goodyear spent most of his life and all of his money perfecting the process of vulcanizing rubber.

1846

OLD SEWING MACHINE

Elias Howe designs the first practical sewing machine, which makes it possible for people to make garments much faster than by hand. This invention changed women's lives forever since prior to that time all stitching was done manually.

ELEVATOR DOOR

1853

A safety break for elevators is created by Elisha Otis. Because of this invention, elevators became safer and it was possible for taller buildings including skyscrapers to be constructed.

1856

Henry Bessemer develops a new process for creating inexpensive steel for all types of construction and industrial applications.

1869

The railroad connecting the east coast to the west coast, the Transcontinental Railroad, is completed in the United States.

TRANSCONTINENTAL RAILROAD

1870

The year 1870 marks the beginning of the Second Industrial Revolution. During this era, new inventions such as the telephone, railways, and the distribution of electrical power expanded the economy and changed transportation and communication.

1876

Alexander Graham Bell creates the first practical form of the telephone.

LIGHT BULB

1877

Workers go on strike on the railways after the railroad companies reduce their wages. Federal troops are called in to curb the violence during what is later called "The Great Railroad Strike."

1879

Thomas Edison and his team succeed in creating the first practical light bulb. Factories soon use electric lighting to create night shifts making it possible to produce more products in less time.

1886

Workers gather together to protect their rights and the American Federation of Labor is established.

1891

The first practical electrical power station is built. It provides energy to the homes and businesses in the central section of London.

ELECTRICAL POWER STATION

OLD AIRPLANE

1903

The Wright Brothers make the very first successful flight with an airplane they built. The flight takes place at a location called Kitty Hawk in North Carolina.

VINTAGE CAR

1908

Henry Ford perfects the assembly line process for building his new car, which he calls the Model T.

1914

World War I begins. This date marks the end of the era of the Industrial Revolution.

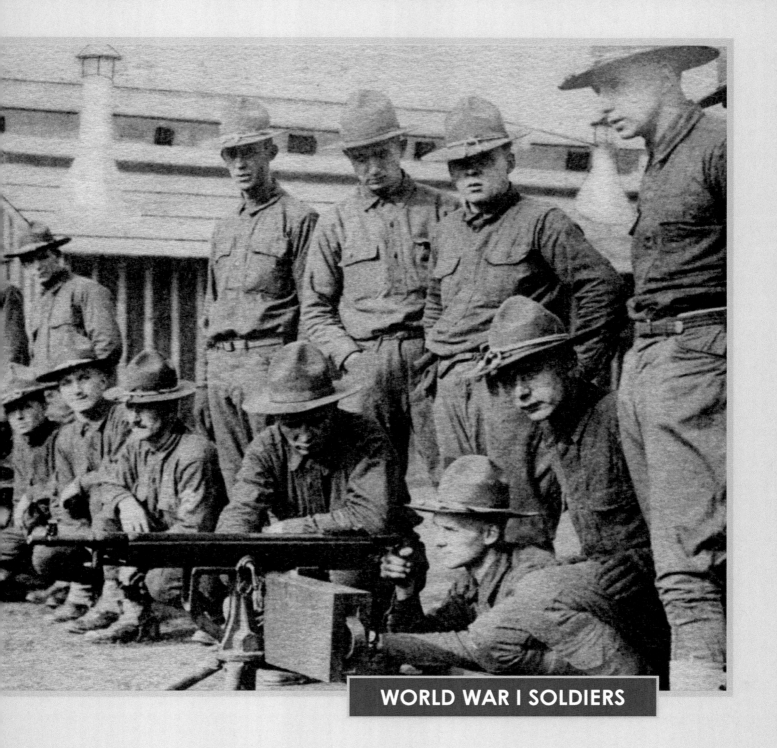

WORLD WAR I SOLDIERS

SUMMARY

The Industrial Revolution is the name given to an era when manufacturing of goods changed forever. Before this global change, products were created on farms and in cottage industries. Almost all the work was done by hand. However, during this era, the advent of new types of machinery revolutionized the way work was done. As new power sources were developed, huge factories sprung up in urban areas. Although conditions were not good for the workers, the efficiency of creating textiles and other types of products increased dramatically. Transportation and communication changed forever as well with the advent of the railroads, telegraph, and telephone.

Awesome! Now that you've read about the history of the Industrial Revolution, you may want to read about the technology and inventions of that era in the Baby Professor book, *Industrial Revolution: The Rise of the Machines (Technology and Inventions) - History Book 6th Grade | Children's History.*

Made in the USA
Middletown, DE
14 August 2020